LEGENDS AND FOLKLORE OF SCOTLAND

By R. S. Holland

BRADWELL
BOOKS

Published by Bradwell Books

9 Orgreave Close Sheffield S13 9NP

Email: books@bradwellbooks.co.uk

British Library Cataloguing in Publication Data: a catalogue record for this book is available from the British Library.

1st Edition

ISBN: 9781909914988

Print: Berforts Information Press. Eynsham. OX29 4JB

Design by: Andrew Caffrey

Typesetting by: Mark Titterton

Photograph Credits: IStock and the author

Cover Photographs
Background image: Shutterstock/ Panos Karas
Green man image: Shutterstock/ Gwoeii
Castle: IStock

CONTENTS

Edinburgh Castle is just one of Scotland's many haunted historic buildings.

INTRODUCTION

The proud nation of Scotland has a heritage of folklore that is all its own. Never conquered by the Romans, this wild northern land developed a unique culture thanks to the mysterious people known as the Picts, with strong input from the thousands of Irish and Scandinavian people who settled here from over the sea.

In this book, you will enjoy a taster of Scotland's wealth of local legends, yarns and strange superstitions. Many tales are told about real historical characters, like Robert the Bruce, St Columba and the courageous 'Black Agnes', who saw off medieval besiegers with extraordinary coolness. Others, like Thomas the Rhymer and King Arthur, are semi-legendary.

Centuries ago, however, people living in the Scottish countryside firmly believed in the existence of characters most of us would certainly consider mythical today. They included fairies, witches and a host of strange and dangerous creatures like the Hogboon, Nuckelavee and the vampire-like Baobhan Sith. Scotland also has an eerie haunted heritage, with many ghost stories told about creepy old castles, ancient houses and even mountaintops and moorland. Edinburgh is considered one of the most haunted cities in the world.

Medieval wizard Michael Scot was buried at Melrose Abbey and his spirit is said to still linger here.

IStock Photo

Sir Walter Scott was responsible for collecting and popularizing a wealth of Scottish folklore and legends.

IStock Photo

Scottish folk tales do more than just hint at the beliefs and customs of our ancestors. They also tell of a Scotland that's full of wonder, magic and mystery, and of lives that were lived larger than life. I hope you enjoy this expedition into the 'gloaming'.

KINGS AND HEROES

More has been written about the legendary King Arthur than any other figure in British folklore. Many claim that his origins are Welsh; others site him in the south-west of England. But there is also a strong tradition of Arthurian lore in Scotland. A recent book, *Finding Arthur* by Adam Ardrey, argues that he was Arthur MacAeden, son of a sixth-century king of Scotland. Mr Ardrey placed his court of Camelot in Argyll, his final battle near Falkirk and named the holy island of Iona (see the next chapter) as his last resting place, the isle of Avalon.

Another theory is that Arthur was a Christian warrior in the Roman army stationed in Scotland who fought to keep back the pagan Picts after the Romans left Britain. In this version of events, Camelot becomes 'Camelon', a fortress that allegedly existed along the Antonine Wall. Geoffrey of Monmouth, the Norman historian who did much to propagate the Arthurian myth, states that he fought one of his important battles at 'Lake Lomand', which has naturally been identified by many as Loch Lomond. There is also a Loch Arthur, south-west of Dumfries, and this has been claimed as the place where the king was presented with his sword, Excalibur.

There are other local traditions regarding King Arthur and his court. His wife, Queen Guinevere, is said to have travelled north to Meigle, near Perth, after Arthur's death and lived the rest of her life here. The King's Knot, an unusual feature in the grounds of Stirling Castle, has long been linked with the Round Table, which Arthur designed to ensure no knight sat higher or lower than any other. Although the Knot resembles a Tudor rose more than anything else, recent geophysics work has demonstrated that a round feature of unknown origin predated it. The most prominent landmark of all is the volcanic crag which towers above Edinburgh. This has been known as Arthur's Seat since the 15th century, but it is thought to be named after a local bigwig rather than the legendary king.

Tradition also suggests that King Arthur's wizard, Merlin, was active in Scotland. He finds his origin in Welsh tradition as Myrddin, a man with the gift of prophecy who was adviser to a nobleman called Gwenddoleu, whom some scholars place as living and fighting in Northern England and the Scottish Borders. After Gwenddoleu died, Myrddin went walkabout around Scotland. Geoffrey of Monmouth changed Myrddin's name to Merlin. Merlin is said to have chummed up with St Mungo, whom he regularly puzzled with his crazy prophecies. One of his prophecies was about his own death. Merlin's Grave has been an important landmark at Drumelzier, near Peebles, for centuries (see the chapter on 'Tam Lin and Thomas the Rhymer').

The Antonine Wall – location of the King Arthur legend?

IStock Photo

Arguably, Scotland's most famous historic king is Robert the Bruce. Robert took the Scottish throne in 1306 and immediately found himself fighting the invading forces of the English king, Edward I. After six long years of war, Robert the Bruce began to despair of being able to hold on to his kingdom.

In the midst of this turmoil there supposedly occurred an incident which, simple and undramatic through it was, has become one of Scotland's most enduring legends. The dejected Robert the Bruce was hiding from the English forces in a cave, overwhelmed by the odds stacked against him. As he languished in despair, his eye was caught by the sight of a small spider attempting to weave a web near the entrance. Time and time again it spun a thread to begin its task, only to fall as the silk broke. Eventually, however, it succeeded: the thread held and the spider was able to complete its web.

Robert was inspired by the little creature's determination and ultimate success. He realised that the only solution to his difficulties was to 'try, try and try again'! He roused himself, continued his campaign of guerrilla warfare and enjoyed a decisive victory at the Battle of Bannockburn in 1314.

That at least is the story, as written by Sir Walter Scott in his series of *Tales of a Grandfather*, published in instalments between 1828 and 1830. Scott is not only Scotland's greatest novelist, he is also an important figure in the collection and promotion of his homeland's folk tales. The legend of Robert the Bruce and the spider has become well known around the world, even though it looks as though Scott borrowed it from a memorial of another Scottish hero, Sir James 'The Black' Douglas. In a history of the Douglas family published in 1643, it is stated that Sir James, who was also fighting the English in Robert the Bruce's time, was inspired to keep going by the sight of a struggling spider. He supposedly told his followers:

> *'I spied a spider climbing by his webb to the height of an trie [tree] and at 12 several times I perceived his web broke, and the spider fel to the ground. But the 13 tyme he attempted and clambe up the tree ...'*

This literary sleight of hand has not prevented several caves from being labelled as the very one where Robert the Bruce watched the indomitable arachnid. They include King Robert the Bruce's Cave near Lockerbie; Bruce's Cave at Balquhidder Glen, Sterling; and the King's Cave at Drumadoon on the Isle of Arran. In addition there is a Bruce's Cave on Rathlin Island, off the northernmost tip of Northern Ireland.

A statue of Robert the Bruce with, in the background, the Wallace Monument. Each commemorates a hero of the wars against Edward I in the 14th century.

iStock Photo

Freedom fighter William Wallace, broadly a contemporary of Robert the Bruce, became even more famous following the *Braveheart* movie released in 1995. *Braveheart* has been criticised for its historical inaccuracies but in truth little is known of Wallace (or 'The Wallace', as he was originally known). Most of what we do know comes from a long poem written well over a century after Wallace's death by an author with the evocative name of Blind Harry. An air of romanticism informs the poem, with The Wallace experiencing one or two prophetic dreams, but otherwise the only aspect of him that can be considered legendary is his supposedly prodigious height. It is claimed he approached seven feet tall. The only support for this assertion is the existence of a broadsword, now on display at the Wallace Monument near Sterling, which, at over five feet in length, would certainly require a strapping man to wield it.

My favourite character from this violent period of Scottish history is the Countess of Dunbar and March. Known as Black Agnes because of her olive skin and raven hair, the Countess was left in charge of Dunbar Castle, East Lothian, while her husband was fighting the English on behalf of King David II. In January 1338, the castle was besieged by William Montagu, 1st Earl of Salisbury. Despite having no more resources to draw on than a skeleton crew of guardsmen and a few servants and ladies-in-waiting, Black Agnes successfully defended Dunbar Castle against the besiegers for six months.

The Earl of Salisbury bombarded the castle with rocks fired by catapults. According to a story that may or may not be apocryphal (and I rather hope it isn't), the Countess and her ladies made a habit of appearing on the battlements after every attack and, with white linen cloths, 'dusting' the areas of smashed masonry. This display of feminine insouciance must have infuriated the besiegers below. Getting nowhere with their catapults, the English forces then brought in a battering ram, to smash through the castle gates. With the same degree of irony, Agnes's meagre company retaliated by heaving back over the battlements the largest of the boulders that had been thrown their way. Scoring a direct hit, it smashed the battering ram to pieces. In June, the disgruntled Earl of Salisbury gave up the siege as a bad job, leaving Black Agnes and her gallant band victorious.

Black Agnes and her ladies show contempt for the English forces besieging Dunbar Castle.

HOLY LORE

The patron saint of Scotland is, of course, St Andrew, brother of St Peter. Tradition states that St Andrew was crucified on a cross in the shape of an 'X'. In heraldry a cross of this shape is known as a 'saltire' and is associated with St Andrew. It appears on the Scottish national flag in white on a blue ground.

According to legend, many of St Andrew's relics were brought from Constantinople to Scotland by St Rule, who experienced a vision in which he was told to keep them safe by taking them to 'the ends of the earth'. This is the reason Andrew became Scotland's national saint. Unfortunately, the relics appear to have been destroyed during the Scottish Reformation. In the 19th century a fragment of St Andrew's shoulder blade was presented to St Mary's Roman Catholic Cathedral in Edinburgh. In 1969 further relics were donated to the cathedral by Pope John VI.

The story behind Scotland's national flag recalls several legends of warriors who are given a sign from God before a victorious battle. The Roman Emperor Constantine, for example, is said to have converted from paganism after seeing a Christian symbol in the setting sun. St Andrew is said to have appeared to King Angus of the Picts on the eve of a battle against the King of Northumbria in AD 832. Angus had joined forces with the king of the Scots, Eochaidh, in a fight to wrest control of Lothian from the Northumbrians. On the morning of the battle itself, Angus saw a white X-shaped cross hanging in a clear blue sky and took this as an encouraging sign from St Andrew. After the Northumbrians were defeated, the Picts and Scots adopted the white saltire on a blue ground as their flag. The battle was fought at a place still named after the vanquished Northumbrian king: Athelstaneford.

St Columba is probably the most famous of Scotland's early saints, although he was originally from Ireland. In AD 561 an undignified row about the ownership of a book with one of his teachers, St Finnian, turned nasty and many men were killed when a fight broke out between the saints' supporters. Feeling partly to blame, Columba decided to exile himself, with a view to saving as many souls as he could in Scotland. St Columba is credited with performing a number of miracles, including seeing into the future, healing and casting out demons. One story has him bringing back to life a dead child. Columba is also said to have seen off the Loch Ness Monster (see the chapter on 'Nessie and Other Water Monsters').

The saltire was much in evidence during the recent campaign for Scottish independence. The flag is said to have been adopted after a vision by King Angus in the ninth century.

IStock Photo

St Columba is most associated with the island of Iona in the Inner Hebrides. Just off the coast of Mull, tiny Iona was a holy place even before St Columba founded a community of monks here in the sixth century. Some sixty ancient Scottish, Irish and Scandinavian kings have been buried on Iona, testimony to Columba's reputation in the so-called Dark Ages and beyond. Today the medieval abbey which superseded Columba's monastery can be visited, along with the ruins of a medieval nunnery. Also present are a number of monumental High Crosses, more than a thousand years old. You might also like to visit the Well of Eternal Youth, blessed by St Brigid, but its properties are open to conjecture.

In addition to the early Columban community, there have been Benedictine and Augustinian monks on Iona and the island is now said to be haunted by veritable hosts of ghostly monks. They are sometimes said to be accompanied by twinkling blue lights. Another odd phenomenon recorded on Iona is the apparition of three mysterious columns of smoke, which rose into the sky from no appreciable source. Fairies are also said to have been encountered on Iona.

Perhaps the best-known story from this mystical place, however, is the so-called 'time slip' allegedly experienced by a Mr MacMillan and related to author Alasdair Alpin MacGregor. Mr MacMillan explained that one moonlit evening he was strolling above White Sands beach when he began to realise that the landscape roundabout had changed. The farm he had been heading towards had vanished, and so too had a number of other landmarks. Glancing across the ocean below, he was even more astonished to see, scudding over the moonlit waves, more than a dozen Viking longboats!

Mr MacMillan could see men rowing and others standing and apparently shouting out in exaltation, but the dramatic scene was

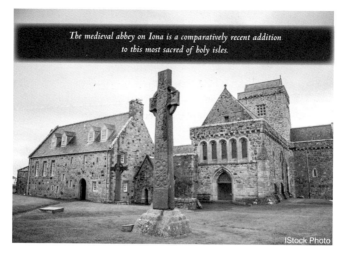

The medieval abbey on Iona is a comparatively recent addition to this most sacred of holy isles.

IStock Photo

played out in silence. When the boats came ashore, the men leaped out, splashing – silently – in the water and hauling them onto the sands. From out of nowhere, a host of monks had appeared behind Mr MacMillan. They went to meet the Danes but were cut down in a fury by the invaders. Mr MacMillan remained frozen to the spot, unable to move or cry out as the murders were committed. Then the Vikings crossed the beach and disappeared inland over the headland. At this point, the witness came out of his spell and everything took on a 20th-century guise again.

After a subsequent visit to the British Museum, Mr MacMillan identified a number of emblems he had seen painted on the sides of the longboats as belonging to the Danish marauders of the tenth century. It is known that Iona was sacked by the Vikings in AD 989 AD (and had been on many occasions prior to that raid).

Another holy site with a great deal of legend attached to it is Rosslyn Chapel, south of Edinburgh. One of these is of very recent date. *The Da Vinci Code*, Dan Brown's bestselling thriller published in 2003, cites Rosslyn Chapel as the final resting place of the Holy Grail. In 1982 Michael Baigent, Richard Leigh and Henry Lincoln had published *The Holy Blood and the Holy Grail*, which attempted to trace Jesus Christ's bloodline through the ages. This and a subsequent work claimed that the Sinclair family, who commissioned the chapel in the 15th century, were descendants of Jesus and Mary Magdalene.

It's all rather far-fetched but visitor numbers to the chapel skyrocketed after the publication of *The Da Vinci Code*. Whatever you think of the Holy Grail connection, Rosslyn Chapel is well worth a visit for the reason that had already made it a popular tourist attraction: it is extraordinarily beautiful. Almost every inch of the interior showcases the exquisite work of the master masons who were specially imported from France to create it in the 15th century. And there is a genuine legend about Rosslyn Chapel. An exceptionally well-carved pillar is said to have been carved by an apprentice while his master was away in Rome. When the master mason returned, he was so overcome with envy at the skill displayed by his protégé that he killed him in a jealous rage. The pillar is now called the Apprentice Pillar. A separate carving, showing a man, a youth and a weeping woman, is pointed out as representing the mason, his apprentice and the boy's grieving mother.

ROBERT KIRK AND THE FAIRIES

Throughout the British Isles, and further afield, there was for centuries a firm belief in a separate order of beings, human in appearance and customs, who regularly visited our world but were not part of it. Generically, they were known as the fairies.

In Scotland the fairies went by a number of names and appeared in many forms. Broadly speaking they were separated into two groups – the Seelie Court, who were graceful, often aristocratic and generally well disposed towards humanity, and the Unseelie, who were grotesque and usually malevolent. Seelie means 'blessed'. The Seelie would always repay a kindness, often with considerable generosity. After a poor woman in the Highlands gave a fairy a quantity of meal, even though she had barely enough to eat herself, she found that her meal-bin remained topped up throughout the forthcoming winter. Other poor people favoured by the fairies for their cleanliness and good manners might be presented with gifts of bread and corn during lean periods.

A number of people claimed to be on excellent terms with the Seelie Court. The most interesting was Robert Kirk, the minister of Aberfoyle, a pretty village in the Trossachs, during the 17th century. In 1691 he wrote a fascinating book called *The Secret Commonwealth of Elves, Fauns and Fairies*. As a native of the village, a trusted clergyman and a speaker of the Gaelic language, Kirk was uniquely placed to record the beliefs and folklore that were fast disappearing from even remote corners of the British Isles during the 17th century. Increasingly repressive forms of Protestantism and the rise of a scientific orthodoxy combined to erode cultural beliefs that had been cherished for centuries. People like Kirk were determined to preserve them while there was still time.

However, *The Secret Commonwealth* is more than just a collection of folk beliefs held by his neighbours. Kirk gives every impression of believing in fairies himself. For him, they were spirits inhabiting a world close to our own but distinct from it. A year after he wrote his book (which wasn't, in fact, published until the 19th century), Kirk died. His body was found lying on the Fairy Knowe, a large mound behind the church. The local Seelie Court was thought to lie beneath the Fairy Knowe, hence its name, and rumour spread that Kirk was not in fact dead, but had been captured by the fairies in revenge for his writing about them and giving away their secrets.

Throughout Britain fairies were believed to be able to substitute real people with wooden facsimiles, known as 'stocks'. Usually stocks were employed when infants were stolen. As a 'changeling', the stock would remain animated, disguising the theft of the real baby from the mother until they'd made sure of their getaway. Some people in Aberfoyle believed that the body found on the Knowe was actually one of these facsimiles and that Kirk himself was waiting to return from the Seelie Court. He now became a figure in a folk tale of his own, one which was still being told after the minister's death.

Sir Walter Scott repeats the tale in his *Letters on Demonology and Witchcraft*, published in 1830. Kirk's spirit appeared just after his first child had been born. He said that he would be permitted to appear again at the christening of his child, and begged that his friend Grahame of Duchray take out his knife and throw it over his (Kirk's) head. Iron and steel are inimical to the fairies and this action would free him: he would be able to return to be a father to his child, a husband to his grieving widow and a minister again to his parish. At the christening feast, Kirk's spirit appeared again but Grahame was so stunned that he failed to draw his dirk in time. Kirk vanished, wailing away, to be a prisoner in the Seelie Court for evermore.

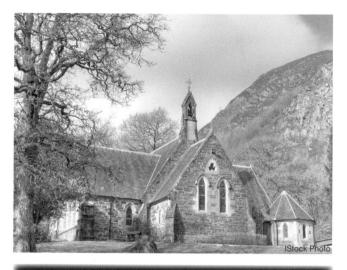

The church at Aberfoyle. A former minister of the village is rumoured to have been captured by fairies after becoming too curious about them.

THE FAIRY FLAG AND CUP

Dunvegan Castle, on the Isle of Skye, is the ancestral home of the Chiefs of the Clan MacLeod. Aside from its important place in Scottish history, its magnificent gothic architecture and its stunning location towering over Loch Dunvegan, the castle is notable for possessing not one but two fairy artefacts. There are several old homes in the British Isles associated with beautiful objects believed to be former possessions of the fairies. Perhaps the best-known example in England is the Luck of Edenhall, a medieval beaker of Venetian glass originally kept at Eden Hall in Cumbria but now in the Victoria and Albert Museum. However, I'm fairly sure that Dunvegan Castle is the only place laying claim to two.

The Fairy Flag is a fragment of much frayed and faded yellow silk with red spots. It was also decorated with little red crosses, but these faded out of existence a century or so ago. The flag's true origin is something of a mystery but one theory is that it was brought back from the Middle East by a Crusading knight. But it may be even older than that, perhaps dating back to as long ago as the fourth century.

Whatever its history, folklore insists the flag is of fairy origin and that it was imbued with magical powers. There are several legends to account for its presence in Dunvegan Castle. One is that an ancestor of the MacLeods married a fairy woman but they had to part when she gave birth to their first son. She wrapped the

Dunvegan Castle, home of the clan MacLeod and two objects said to have originally belonged to the fairies.

child in the flag and returned to fairyland. Another has it that a fairy woman entered the castle of her own volition and wrapped it round the infant heir of the MacLeods to magically protect him from harm. It is said that for centuries afterwards the flag was incorporated into the bedclothes of all future heirs (which might explain its tattered condition). The final story is that the Crusading MacLeod met a fairy woman in the Holy Land and she gave him the flag. This may be a case of a legend trying to square with historical fact.

Beyond its role of protection, tradition has it the Fairy Flag has performed many miracles. On two occasions, according to the legend, unfurling it has resulted in the magical creation of hordes of armed men to swell the ranks of the MacLeods when they were threatened by rival clans. Twice the flag has been employed for this purpose, but there is a ban on it being used a third time because this would result in the return of the flag to fairyland or, in a grimmer version of the story, an appalling calamity befalling the clan MacLeod.

The Fairy Flag has also been credited with having cured members of the MacLeod family of a variety of illnesses. It has also been used to cure the clan's cattle of a plague. Not only that, but it is said to have the ability to boost the fertility of humans and livestock and to attract herring into the loch!

The other fairy artefact held at the castle is the Dunvegan Cup. This is a communal or ceremonial beaker dating from the 15th century. It is made of wood richly ornamented with silver filigree, silver gilt and niello, a black alloy popular in the Middle Ages. The cup is a strange shape, at least to modern eyes, but very beautiful and it's no wonder legend has built up around it.

The legend of the Dunvegan Cup is that it came into the possession of a member of the MacLeod family after he spotted a troop of fairies gambolling outside a ruined broch called Dun Osdale (a broch is a stone tower erected by the Picts during the Dark Ages). The fairies invited him in and offered him a drink from an elaborate vessel. Tasting fairy food and drink can be dangerous – it can put you in their power – so the canny fellow only pretended

An old postcard of the Fairy Flag and the Dunvegan Cup at Dunvegan Castle, along with another relic of the MacLeods, Sir Rory Mor's Horn.

to take a drink. Then he made his escape, carrying the cup away with him.

The fairies were understandably furious and they put a curse on the cup. They imbued it with the fairy magic called 'glamour' so that anyone who saw it would be overcome by an unconquerable desire to possess it. When the new owner began to show off his booty, one of his friends killed him for it. The horrified Chief of the MacLeods took charge of the cup and, having caught and hanged the murderer, kept it safely out of harm's way in Dunvegan Castle (where, of course, he could enjoy it himself!).

Today the Fairy Flag and the Dunvegan Cup can still be seen at Dunvegan Castle. The accompanying photo of the two artefacts was taken at Dunvegan in the 1920s. The picture shows another relic of the clan, a medieval drinking horn that belonged to Sir Rory Mor MacLeod, the 15th chief of the clan.

TAM LIN AND THOMAS THE RHYMER

One of the most striking Scottish folk tales is that of Young Tam Lin or Tamlane. The story survives in ballad form and is full of vivid imagery and fairy-lore. The legend was told in the Borders and Aberdeenshire and centres on Carterhaugh, near Selkirk. It begins with a warning from the laird of Carterhaugh to his daughter, Janet, about a strange being, named Tam Lin, who haunts the neighbouring woodland. Now that she has become a young woman, she must stay away from Carterhaugh Woods, for Tam Lin will be sure to appear and claim her maidenhood.

Full of curiosity, the impetuous Janet disobeys her father's command and sneaks out to an old well in the wood. There she plucks a double rose and in so doing inadvertently summons Tam Lin, a handsome but unearthly youth. Tam Lin asks why she is trespassing in his wood and why she has taken something that therefore belongs to him. Janet pertly replies that the woods belong to her father and that he has given them to her. Tam Lin claims his bounty nonetheless and Janet returns to her father's castle pregnant but not, it has to be said, unhappy.

When Janet can keep her condition a secret no longer, she admits the origin of her unborn child but at first insists that she will keep it. Pressure from her family forces her to seek a termination and she is told of a herb growing in the woods which will bring this about. Reluctantly, she returns to the forest in search of it, but when she plucks the plant from the ground Tam Lin reappears. He demands to know why she is intending to take this drastic act. In response, the emotionally torn Janet asks him who he is: is he a Christian, is he even human?

Tam Lin explains that he is the grandson of the Thane of Roxburgh. One day he was out riding in the woods when he fell from his horse. He was immediately captured by the Queen of the Fairies, who dragged him into a mound and from there down to fairyland. Now, although he can visit the woodland, he is enchanted and belongs to fairyland. He goes on to say that it is the custom on Hallowe'en night once every seven years for the Queen of the Fairies to make a tithe of one mortal man to hell. Tonight is Hallowe'en and he is afraid that it is his turn to be sacrificed. But if Janet loves him and wants to save him, there is a chance.

> *Just at the mirk and midnight hour, the fairy folk will ride,' he tells her. 'And they that wad their true-love win, at Miles Cross they maun bide.'*

Tam Lin explains that he will be one of the company of fairies riding past Miles Cross at midnight. He will be on the third horse, a white one. If Janet can grab him and drag him from his horse there, the enchantment will be broken and he will belong to her and no longer to the Fairy Queen. He warns Janet that the task won't be easy: in order to prevent Janet claiming him, the fairies will transform him into a number of unpleasant forms.

> *'They'll turn me in your arms, lady, into an esk [a newt] and adder,' he says, 'but hold me fast, and fear me not, I am your bairn's father.'*

Finally, says Tam, they will transform him into a molten blob of iron ('a red het gaud of airn'), so that Janet will have no choice but to drop him, but if she keeps her head and throws the cinder into the nearby well he will immediately become a mortal man again, free of the Fairy Queen's power. Everything falls out as Tam Lin

A 19th-century illustration of Tam Lin first appearing to Janet in the woods at Carterhaugh.

Eildon Hill, where Thomas the Rhymer encountered the Fairy Queen. King Arthur and his Knights are said to sleep under this hill. Tradition states that the three peaks were created from a single one by a demon.

IStock Photo

predicted and brave Janet succeeds in holding onto her lover until he is transformed into a cinder, which she throws into the well. Tam Lin emerges as a 'naked knight'. Janet wraps him in her green mantle.

The Queen of the Fairies is furious: 'She's taen awa the bonniest knight in a' my companie,' she complains, and says that if she'd known Tam Lin had eyes for another woman she'd have replaced them with ones made of wood. However, she has to admit defeat and Janet and Tam Lin return to Carterhaugh, where they are married. Janet gives birth to a beautiful son and they all live – of course – happily ever after.

Another mortal man who supposedly had dealings with the Queen of the Fairies was Thomas of Erceldoune, also known as Thomas the Rhymer and True Thomas. Thomas was a real person, a thane in the Scottish Borders in the 13th century. He must have been a remarkable man, for within a hundred years of his death, legends had built up around him and these were in print by the 15th century. As well as being a poet, Thomas had the reputation of being a seer and a prophet.

Tradition has it that Thomas the Rhymer was given the gift of prophecy by the Fairy Queen. Thomas was wandering on Eildon Hill, an anciently inhabited mountain with a mystical reputation, when the Queen of Elfland spotted him and immediately fell in love. Like Tam Lin, Thomas found himself carried off to fairyland. He served as the Queen's servant — and perhaps more — for seven years. The Queen then let him return to the mortal world so that he would avoid the risk of being chosen for the tithe of hell. In addition to his prophetic powers, the Queen bestowed upon him something of a mixed blessing, a tongue that could not lie (hence his nickname of True Thomas).

Among his prophecies Thomas is said to have accurately predicted the crowning of James the VI of Scotland as James I of England, thereby uniting the two nations. The prophecy stated that: 'When Tweed and Powsail meet at Merlin's grave, Scotland and England shall one monarch have.' On the day of James's coronation, the River Tweed flooded the Powsail Burn at a place near the village of Drumelzier where Merlin was popularly believed to have been buried.

In old age, Thomas the Rhymer returned to fairyland. While he was enjoying a feast at his castle, a messenger ran in and breathlessly announced that a stag and a doe had left the forest and were stalking majestically towards the castle. Thomas went to meet them and all three turned round and re-entered the forest. He was never seen again, but he does turn up in a few later traditions in which he is now happily ensconced in fairyland, acting as an adviser to the Queen and a mediator between the two worlds.

THE UNSEELIE

The Unseelie is the name sometimes given to the order of numerous and malevolent fairies who at one time troubled the imaginations of the rural Scots. As we have seen, the members of the generally well-disposed Seelie Court could be difficult to deal with and their Queen had the habit of capturing good-looking young men who caught her fancy. But its Unseelie equivalent, the Sluagh, or 'Host', were far more dangerous: they would capture people and then press gang them into fighting for them or carrying out wicked deeds against mankind.

As late as the 1940s, researcher Alexander MacGregor was able to find someone on the Isle of Skye who was sufficiently concerned about the wiles of malicious fairies that he never failed to ask to be protected from them in his prayers. The nightly prayer offered up by the elderly Mr Farquhar Beaton is reprinted in MacGregor's *Highland Superstitions*:

'O Blessed One, provide for us and help us, and let not thy grace fall on us like rain-drops on the back of a goose. When a man is in danger on the point of a promontory at sea, do thou succour him; and be about and with us on dry land. Preserve the aged and the young, our wives and our children, our sheep and our cattle, from the power and dominion of the fairies, and from the malicious effects of every evil eye. Let a straight path be before us, and a

The Mousa Broch in Shetland. These ruined Pictish fortifications were said to be the haunt of a strange being known as the Kunal-Trow.

IStock Photo

happy end to our journey.'

Asked why a man of the 20th century would still believe in fairies, Mr Beaton tersely replied: 'My own two eyes beheld them; my two ears heard them.'

In the Shetland Isles, the fairies were known as 'trows' and were described as short, squat and ugly. They lived in ancient burial mounds and were only active during the night, which suggests that the islanders originally considered them spirits of the dead. Often they were invisible, or visible only to those with 'second sight'. Those without the gift could only see them if they held hands with, or placed their foot over the foot of, someone who had it. They might then be amazed by the great crowds of trows swarming around them.

After dark, trows were regular visitors to crofters' homes. They would warm themselves by the glowing embers of the fire but might prove unwelcome guests by making a din. It's somewhat surprising that they should bother visiting humble crofts, for their own subterranean homes were said to be luxurious, crammed with gold and glittering gemstones. They were mightily fond of music, and musicians were at particular risk of being abducted by them. During the Christmas season, the trows had special dispensation to visit the earth, even during daylight, so Shetlanders were especially wary of them at midwinter. Uttering some holy words or showing the cross was usually enough to get rid of a trow, however. Also, when visible, they became frozen to the spot and unable to move all the time one kept one's eye on them.

The Kunal-Trow was a kind of King of the Trows. Described as looking like a very old man, the Kunal-Trow had his home in the ruins of the Pictish round towers known as 'brochs'. At times he would venture abroad in search of a wife among the Shetlanders. Unfortunately, his chosen bride would always die as soon as she had given birth to his child (invariably a son). This was not only bad news for his wife but was also sad for the Kunal-Trow, who as a result lived a sad and lonely existence.

Orkney folklore tells of beings similar to the trows called variously 'hogboons', 'hogboys' or 'hugboys'. The name comes from the Old Norse for 'mound-dweller' or 'mound-farmer'. They too made their home in prehistoric burial mounds, including the most impressive in the Orkney Islands, Maeshowe. When Maeshowe was being excavated in 1862, the archaeologist in charge, James Farrer, noted: 'The country people state that [Maeshowe] was formerly inhabited by a person named Hogboy, possessing great strength.'

Hogboons were much more dangerous than their Shetland equivalents. They would instantly strike dead anyone trying to dig into their homes in search of treasure. Even allowing your cattle to graze on the grass growing over their mounds would be enough for them to exact revenge.

Mr W.E. Thorner claimed to have seen trow-like beings on the Orkney island of Hoy while he was stationed there during the Second World War. In the 1960s he wrote to a Scottish magazine about his experience and his letter is quoted on the excellent orkneyjar.com website run by Orcadian Sigurd Towrie:

'One stormy day in winter I was walking or struggling along the cliff top at Torness. The wind was high and howled about, low-lying, swirling clouds part-enveloped the land in misty rain. At times the pressure was so great that I was forced to bend and clutch at the heather to retain a footing.

Maeshowe, the best known of Orkney's prehistoric burial mounds, was one of those where the malevolent hogboons had their home.

IStock Photo

'On one such occasion, on looking up I was amazed to see that I had the company of what appeared to be a dozen or more "wild men" dancing about, to and fro. These creatures were small in stature ... they possessed round faces, sallow in complexion, with long, dark, bedraggled hair. As they danced about, seeming to throw themselves over the cliff edge, I felt that I was a witness to some ritual dance of a tribe of primitive men.

'It is difficult to describe in a few words my feelings at this juncture or my bewilderment. The whole sequence could have lasted about three minutes until I was able to leave the cliff edge.'

The hogboons were among the most dangerous members of the Unseelie but there were others just as deadly. The Brown Man of the Muirs, for example, broadly resembled his Orkney and Shetland cousins in being ugly and short in stature. Katharine Briggs, in her essential *Dictionary of Fairies*, adds that he is dressed in an outfit 'the colour of withered bracken' and boasts 'great glowing eyes like a bull'. The Brown Man was inimical to humans but looked after all the birds and animals on the moors; he targeted anyone hunting or shooting them.

One day in 1744, according to an allegedly true story told to Sir Walter Scott, two young men encountered the Brown Man of the Muirs while out hunting on a moor near Elsdon in the Borders. They were taking a rest beside a burn when, looking up, they saw him standing on the other side, waving his fist and berating them for shooting his hares and grouse. The Brown Man told them that they should be like him and eat only nuts, apples and whortleberries. Apparently growing calmer, he then invited the huntsmen to come with him to his home so that they could try out the vegan diet for themselves.

One of the young men was happy to take up his invitation and was about to leap the burn when his friend shouted at him to stop. The Brown Man would surely have torn him to pieces if he had jumped over. Unable to cross the running water and reach the youths, the infuriated Brown Man vanished. The more impetuous of the two friends, however, shrugged off the warning and made even more effort to shoot the game on the moor. Shortly afterwards he became ill and died – in consequence, it was thought, of his defiance of the Brown Man of the Muirs.

The Baobhan Sith (pronounced 'bavan shee') was a species of vampire which haunted the wild Highlands. In one tale, four young men out hunting on the moors in Wester Ross escaped the attentions of the Brown Man of the Muirs but met with an equally unpleasant fate. At nightfall they took shelter in a sheep-hut and one of them wished for female company to dance with. The others sighed in agreement – and then four young women suddenly sauntered through the door. One of the men played the jew's harp while the others danced. As they circled round the little hut, the musician noticed that blood was dripping from his friends, and the fourth girl was approaching him with a hungry look in her eyes.

The young man ran out of the hut, pursued by the shrieking Baobhan Sith. He got among the horses, which somehow protected him but the vampire prowled round and round him all night. She vanished at dawn. When the boy went to check on his friends, he found them lifeless on the ground, the blood drained from their bodies.

The Dwarfie Stane on Hoy in Orkney is the remains of a Neolithic tomb. It was believed to be haunted by the man buried here and it is the ideal home for a hogboon.

SEA FAIRIES

In addition to the Seelie and Unseelie courts, Scottish folklore is rich in stories of fairies who lived in the sea. Not surprisingly, these traditions were most strong in Orkney, Shetland and the Hebrides. The best-known order of Scottish sea-going fairies were the 'selkies', who were believed to live as seals in the sea but who would shed their skins on dry land and become humanoid. They were also known as 'the Roane'.

Selkies were very sexual beings. The males were said to be devastatingly handsome and possessed of an animal magnetism mortal women found hard to resist. The lonesome wives of fishermen who spent months on end at sea were especially vulnerable to their charms. Sometimes the selkie didn't need to make any of the running: a lonely or disappointed woman seeking a selkie husband only needed to weep seven tears into the sea to summon one.

The females were less interested in human beings but were very beautiful, so mortal men often wished to take them as wives. In order to do so, they would look out for selkie women coming ashore at moonlight so that they could then steal their discarded seal skins. Once they had possession of the skin, the selkie was in their power. They would willingly become the human's wife and even bear him children, but would always long for the sea. If she should find her seal skin, a selkie woman would return to the ocean without a second thought. In some tales, her children come across the skin's hiding place and, without knowing its importance, innocently hand it to their mother. Her children's needs make no difference to the selkie: she quits her home with alacrity, and never returns.

Mermaids and mermen also feature in Scottish lore and were the archetypal half-human-half-fish creatures found in folklore everywhere. In Scotland, however, it was believed they were unable to come onto land and could survive out of water no longer than a fish could. One old story from Shetland tells of a selkie who was caught by fishermen and skinned so that she would be in their power. However, the poor naked selkie succeeded in wriggling off their boat and back under the water. There she told a mermaid of her trouble. The mermaid bravely allowed herself to be caught in the nets in the hope that she might be able to convince the fishermen to return the skin to her friend. Her pleas were in vain, however. On the contrary, the men believed she would fetch a good price in the market.

IStock Photo

When grey seals came ashore on the Scottish coastline, some of them turned into selkies.

The cruel fishermen were unaware that terrible storms followed when a member of the merfolk died. The mermaid, however, was well aware of this and realised that her death might do some good for her selkie friend. Lying on the seal skin, she passed away in the open air and at once a violent squall blew up, sinking the fishing boat. The bodies of the drowned men and the courageous mermaid sank to the bottom of the sea, along with the seal skin, which the selkie gratefully donned again.

In 1830 a mermaid was reported as having been killed and afterwards buried on a beach in Benbecula, in the Outer Hebrides. It was described as being about the size of a child of three or four, with long, dark hair, a human face, 'abnormally developed breast' and a lower body resembling a salmon but lacking the scales. It was first spotted by a woman collecting seaweed. It was bobbing about in the water and turning somersaults in a playful manner. A small crowd saw it at play and then some boys threw stones at the creature, and one of them struck her. Its body washed up two miles away a few days later. The remorseful villagers buried the body on the beach and marked its resting place with an upright stone as a marker. This stone can still be seen. Spoilsports from the Commission on the Ancient and Historical Monuments of Scotland, however, have recently examined the site and have identified it as simply a natural formation that hasn't been put there by anyone.

Similar to the selkies were the Orkney Finfolk. The Finfolk were believed to live on two mythical islands called Hildaland and Hether Blether which would appear and disappear at will. The Finfolk were a grim gang of fairies with more than a taint of the black arts about them. They were truly amphibious, as happy in the sea as they were on dry land, and were considered unparalleled mariners. In winter they stayed in Finfolkaheem, their underwater city, returning to trouble the Orkney islanders in the summer.

Sharing a habit associated with malevolent fairies, the Finmen would steal people away to one of their mysterious islands, where they would be forced to dwell for ever as husband or wife to one of their own tribe. The Finwives were quite different: they would settle among the Orkney islanders, telling their fortunes, casting spells and generally extorting money from them. The Finfolk made such a nuisance of themselves that a heroic chap named Thorodale cast them all off Hildaland and Christianised the island. It then became a real, solid island and today is called Eynhallow, or 'Holy Island'.

Sigurd Towrie repeats a puzzling incident which was linked to the legends of the Finfolk as recently as 1990. On his orkneyjar.com website, he writes:

'On Saturday, July 14, 1990, an outing, organised by the Orkney Heritage Society and the Royal Society for the Protection of Birds, landed a number of ferry passengers on the uninhabited island of **Eynhallow** for a short visit. As usual the crew counted the number of passengers upon disembarking. Eighty-eight visitors stepped from the boat and onto the soil of the once magical island. According to the evidence from the crew, only eighty-six returned.

'These two missing passengers sparked off a massive air and sea search. Men from the local police and coastguard scoured the island as well as the coastlines of the islands nearby. To no avail. In the air a helicopter dispatched by the Shetland Coastguard swept the area with their heat-sensing equipment but nothing was found. Needless to say the whole incident was blamed on the ferry crew miscounting the number of passengers but at the time the Chief Inspector of the Kirkwall Police was not so sure. "We have corroborative statements from the crew members ... it's a strange one," he said.

'The Eynhallow incident had some of the older Orcadian folk murmuring about the old ways and whether the missing "tourists" might actually be none other than Finmen returning to their ancient home.'

There is one more seafaring creature in Scottish folklore to consider: the terrifying Nuckelavee. Once again, it is the Orcadians who suffered most from this monster. Katharine Briggs describes the Nuckelavee as 'a kind of hideous centaur, for like a centaur he rose out of a horse's back and had no human legs. He came out of the sea and spread evil wherever he went, blighting crops, destroying livestock and killing every man whom he could encounter.'

Fortunately, the Nuckelavee was strictly a marine animal and couldn't bear fresh water. The only way to escape him was to cross a stream, for the monster would be forced to remain on the other side (in much the same way as the Brown Man of the Muirs in the previous chapter).

IStock Photo

A mermaid allegedly came close to the shore of Benbecula in 1830 but was killed by unthinking schoolboys. The little creature was then buried on the beach where its body was found washed up.

NESSIE AND OTHER WATER MONSTERS

For centuries, we are informed, Loch Ness has harboured a monster. This narrow stretch of water, twenty-three miles long and deeper than the North Sea, extends from just south of Inverness, south-west through the Great Glen. Although rarely seen (if indeed it has ever truly been seen), 'Nessie' has become a major tourist attraction and something of an icon. Many have gone in search of it, often employing cutting-edge technology, but none have found conclusive proof of it, nor have any remains of the monster ever been found along the loch's shore.

The first sighting of the Loch Ness Monster is said to have taken place in the sixth century. St Columba requested one of his followers to swim across a narrow stretch of the loch to fetch over a boat moored on the opposite bank. When the man was halfway across, a huge animal reared out of the water and bore down on the swimmer, roaring hungrily. St Columba shouted back and, in the name of God, ordered the monster to do his follower no harm. 'Go back!' he demanded, and the chastened creature retreated the way it had come. That is pretty much all that was heard of the Loch Ness Monster until the 1930s, when fresh sightings were reported and a photograph allegedly showing the raised neck of the beast caused a sensation in the Press.

Since then more Scottish lochs (and indeed lakes worldwide) have been credited with having their own monster. For example, some believe Loch Morar, in western Highland, is inhabited by 'Morag', a serpentine creature. Sightings of Morag date back to the 1880s, with a dramatic incident supposedly taking place in 1969, when it was accidentally struck by a speedboat and fought back! Loch Morar and Loch Ness both terminate only a mile so from the sea and it has been suggested that subterranean tunnels might provide these creatures with a much larger habitat than the lochs and that they may therefore be only occasional visitors.

The fact remains, however, that a range of mythical lake monsters are prominent in Scottish folklore, and the country's modern-day examples may simply be a continuation of this folk belief. Usually, they take the form of a Water Horse, or, in Gaelic, the 'Each Uisge'. Initially appearing in the form of an especially handsome but otherwise normal horse, the Each Uisge soon reveals itself to be a cruel and savage creature.

This 'horse' would lurk beside lochs just waiting to be caught and ridden. Should anyone be foolish enough to climb on its back, however, they would soon discover they were unable to get off again. It was as if the animal's skin had been coated in superglue. The Water Horse would leap into the loch, bearing its hapless prey with it, and there devour him, rejecting only the liver (perhaps because it tasted too strongly of whisky?). The Each Uisge was a dangerous and powerful animal. In a story from Islay in the Inner Hebrides, a powerful bull was torn apart by one as if it was made of paper. Intriguingly, there is a tradition of an Each Uisge living in Loch Ness. Such a tradition might perhaps have inspired belief in Nessie.

A close cousin of the Each Uisge is the Kelpie. The Kelpie haunted rivers rather than lochs but behaved in a similar way: taking on the disguise of a pony and waiting for somebody to jump up onto his back. Then he would gallop off at a breakneck pace over the

Loch Ness. Does a legendary monster lurk below the surface?

IStock Photo

moors and mountains and down precipices, to the terror of the unfortunate on his back, who was forced to cling on for dear life (the Kelpie's coat was not adhesive like the Each Uisge's). Eventually, the Kelpie would dive into a deep pool in the river and thrash his tail about, creating a noise like thunder. If the human had survived all that, they were usually free to swim to shore – the Kelpie rarely devoured its victims. Although dangerous, a Kelpie could be tamed if a bridle was thrown over his head.

A famous Kelpie lived in Noran Water, the river running beneath Vayne Castle in Angus. So strong was this monster that its mighty hoof made an indelible mark in a slab of sandstone beside the river. Or at least that's what people used to say. In *The History and Traditions of the Land of the Lindsays in Angus and Mearns* (1853), author Andrew Jervise informs his readers:

'A little east of the castle, close by the side of the Noran, a large sandstone has lain from time immemorial, bearing a deep indentation resembling the hoof of a colossal horse with the impress of one of the caulkers of the heel. This has been fashioned by the falling out of a large pebble imbedded in the stone, though at first glance it looks like an artificial work. It is popularly called the Kelpie's Footmark, and was believed to have been occasioned by his step while bounding among the rocks. Some of the largest of these he not only amused himself by overturning when the water was swollen, but, as if conscious of his own unbridled power, he boldly seated himself on others, and called lustily for help, in the feigned voice of a drowning person, so he might lure his victim to the river!'

This latter habit was shared by an even stranger denizen of Scotland's rivers: the Shellycoat. The Shellycoat was so-named for all the shells it had picked up over the years and which had become attached to its coat. The shells made it rattle when it moved. The Shellycoat too enjoyed crying out like a drowning man, but its reason for doing so was no more than mischievous. Whenever anyone ran to the riverside to help, it would leap up and laugh uproariously, thinking this was a huge joke, before swimming away.

Finally, we must consider the Lavellan. I am indebted to cryptozoologist Dr Karl Shuker for informing me of this interesting little beast. According to tradition, certain deep pools and rivers in Caithness were once home to the Lavellan, a kind of giant shrew, much bigger than a rat, which had a venomous bite. In the 18th century the Welsh naturalist Thomas Pennant visited Scotland on one of his many rambles, and hearing of the Lavellan in Ausdale, went in search of it. He failed to find a living specimen but was told that a preserved skin survived at one of the farms, and water in which it had been soaked was used to cure various ailments affecting the livestock. Perhaps the Lavellan was a genuine animal, long since extinct.

IStock Photo

A re-imagining of the famous photo supposedly taken of the Loch Ness Monster in 1933. Witnesses of lake monsters in various parts of the world have often described them as having a 'horse-like head', which might be a link to the Water Horse of legend.

THE FEAR OF WITCHCRAFT

For many centuries, it was believed that misfortune, illness and even death could be willed upon a person by another who was skilled in the mystic arts or who had been given the power to do so by the Devil. Because witchcraft appears in the Bible (for example, in the story of the Witch of Endor and the conjuring up of a demon for King Solomon), the 'dark arts' were believed in as firmly by educated people as the illiterate.

It might seem the height of foolish ignorance to believe in witchcraft, but it should be remembered that prior to the 18th century, almost nothing was understood about the causes of disease. Microbes were unknown. We believe in the virus giving us a cold even though we have never seen it, and our ancestors believed in the existence of witchcraft with the same degree of certainty.

So firm was the belief in witchcraft that someone accused of cursing an animal or human to fall ill or die was treated just the same as if they had murdered their victims by more orthodox means. The criminal justice system saw no difference: the end result was all that mattered. By the dawn of the 17th century, however, Europe had fallen into the grip of a 'witch mania', fuelled in part by the resurgence of bubonic plague and by religious insecurity fanned by the Renaissance. No one was safe from being accused of being a witch. Lonely old women, especially those who had previously been known to provide herbal remedies, harmless love charms and the like, were early targets, but even the nobility found themselves accused, often by the unscrupulous as a means to get them out of the way. Thousands of supposed witches and male sorcerers were hanged or burned alive as the mania swept across Europe.

In Scotland the flames were fanned, almost literally, by its king, James VI (later James I of England). James was an unwavering believer in witchcraft and was convinced there had been several plots made against him by witches and sorcerers (see the next chapter). In 1597 the king wrote a book, *Demonology*, in order to warn his people of the dangers they faced from witchcraft:

> *'The fearful abounding at this time in this country of these detestable slaves of the Devil, the Witches or the Enchanters, has moved me (beloved reader) to dispatch in post this following treatise of mine,' he writes, 'to resolve the doubting hearts of many, both that such assaults of Satan are most certainly practised, and that the instruments thereof merits most severely to be punished.'*

James VI's superstitious dread and his insistence that his representatives actively seek out and execute witches undoubtedly led to the deaths of many innocent people. It was certainly the case when, in 1591, a jury found one Barbara Napier of Edinburgh innocent of the charge of witchcraft. The king personally intervened so that they were forced to change their verdict to 'guilty'. It's likely they simply didn't believe in witchcraft but excused themselves by saying that they couldn't accept the evidence against her, which had exclusively come from other accused witches (their confessions of devil worship no doubt having being forced from them by threat and torture).

James insisted that witchcraft 'is a thing grown very common amongst us'. He continued: 'I know it to be a most abominable sin, and I have occupied for three quarters of this year in laws both of God and men that this sin is most odious … and punishable by death.'

Poor Barbara!

James VI of Scotland, later also James I of England and Wales. King James firmly believed in witches and the power of the dark arts and encouraged similar beliefs in his subjects.

iStock Photo

In 1604, after becoming king of England and Wales as well as of Scotland, James passed more severe laws. Death became the only available punishment for anyone found guilty of practising witchcraft, regardless of the end result of their spells. Previously, the supposed witch would have had to have committed a crime through their witchcraft which would also have warranted capital punishment. With such paranoia prevalent at the very top of society, the stage was set for a rash of accusations and executions. No wonder the canny William Shakespeare wrote a play about Scottish witches in the following decade – he knew how much his *Macbeth* would please the Crown!

By the 1620s, however, King James had drastically altered his opinion on the existence of witches. He grew increasingly dismayed by the number of people hanged on the evidence of children, who would claim to be possessed by devils inflicted on them by their neighbours. According to one contemporary source: 'The frequency of forged possessions wrought such an alteration upon the judgement of King James that … he grew first diffident of, and then flatly to deny, the workings of witches and devils as mere falsehoods and delusions.'

Unfortunately, this did not end the persecutions. It has been estimated that, between 1573 and 1722, more than four thousand men, women and children were executed for witchcraft in Scotland alone. According to commentator John Wagstaffe, in his *The Question of Witchcraft Debated*, published in 1669: 'In no country did the belief persist more lately, in no country did the prosecution of sorcery rage fiercer and the fires blaze brighter than in Scotland.'

SOME SCOTTISH WITCHES AND WIZARDS

An early victim of the Scottish witch trials was Bessie Dunlop, of Dalry, in Ayrshire. The 'Witch o' Dalry', as she became known, was a 'wise woman', what some today might call a white witch, who sold herbal medicines for people and animals and dabbled in fortune telling and other forms of divination. Most rural communities up and down the British Isles had their own wise man or woman. Among their other duties, they would provide charms to attract lovers and – ironically – to ward off witchcraft. Tragically, such savants were among the first to find themselves rounded up in the witch hunts. Bessie ended up being burned at the stake as early as 1576.

Poor Bessie admitted that she cast spells and had as her familiar the ghost of a soldier named Thomas Reid, who had died in the Battle of Pinkie in 1547. His apparition had introduced himself to her one day while she was crossing a field. At the time Bessie's husband, child and only cow were all dangerously ill. The ghost had spoken kindly to her and had correctly predicted that although the animal and her child would perish, her husband would survive. This was the first of many subsequent meetings with Reid's ghost.

Today this channelling of a spirit might be considered mediumship, but it would have been seen as nothing less than necromancy –

Macbeth meets the three witches. In writing his tragedy, Shakespeare tapped into the contemporary dread of witchcraft shared by most of the populace, including the current King, James I.

MACBETH

the conjuring of the dead for the purposes of divination – by Bessie's accusers. Indeed, they may have gone further, assuming that 'Thomas Reid' was actually the Devil in disguise. This would have been confirmed by Bessie's own admission that the ghost had ordered her to renounce Christianity. He also tried to lure her to Fairyland, where he said he usually dwelled. Oddly, Bessie stated that she also saw 'Thomas' walking among mortal people from time to time, both in Edinburgh and in Dalry. Perhaps he wasn't just a figment of her imagination but a real man, possessed of certain arcane knowledge, who had hoodwinked a credulous woman into thinking he was supernatural.

Bessie's testimony does not tally with the usual accounts of devil worship, animal familiars and witches' sabbats that works on demonology and later witch trials would lead us to expect. Bessie appears to be channelling her own folk beliefs rather than anything Satanic. She was probably repeating whatever stories she had told her neighbours to impress them with her power. In subsequent decades those prosecuting alleged witches would doubtless lead their questioning based on what they had 'learned' through works like King James's *Demonology* and extract confessions to such activities through torture. Bessie's prosecution, being so early, perhaps escaped such interference and represents a truer glimpse into the beliefs held by country folk at the time.

In 1590 a trial began which became a sensation and truly kicked off the Scottish witch hunts. When King James was returning from Copenhagen, having married Anne, sister of the King of Denmark, his ship became embroiled in a violent storm. Its captain managed to steer it into safe waters off Norway, where it was able to take shelter. It was shortly afterwards joined by the floundering Danish fleet, which had been escorting the royal ship. During their enforced delay, the Danish admiral told James he believed that the storm had been created by the wife of one of the officials in Copenhagen. He said the woman was suspected of being skilled in the art of sorcery and, moreover, he had unwittingly offended her before the fleet left.

This unlikely story led to a two-year trial of members of the gentry both in Scotland and in Denmark. In addition, more than a hundred ordinary people in North Berwick, East Lothian, found themselves accused as the mania caught hold and neighbour

King James VI of Scotland presides over the North Berwick witch trial. The officer threatening the accused with a stick more than hints at the lack of justice afforded to those finding themselves on trial, to say nothing of the cruelty that was meted out to them.

denounced neighbour. Under torture, many of the accused admitted to belonging to a coven which met at St Andrew's Auld Kirk.

One of these, Agnes Sampson, was examined by King James himself at Holyrood Palace in Edinburgh. This unfortunate woman was tortured until she 'confessed' to fifty-three charges of witchcraft, including attempts to kill the king. Agnes was chained to a wall in a dungeon, kept without sleep and had a 'bridle' thrust into her mouth, piercing her cheeks and tongue with iron spikes. Finally she went through three mock hangings before she broke down and admitted to anything that was put to her. Her reward was death by strangulation, after which her body was burned.

The person identified through these barbaric practices as the leader of the coven was Dr John Fian, a schoolmaster in Prestonpans. The sufferings inflicted on Dr Fian to get him to confess to being Master of the Coven were considerably more severe than those of Agnes Sampson. His nails were torn out with pincers and needles were thrust into his fingertips. His legs were confined in 'boots' which were used to crush his feet. We are informed that his 'bones and flesh [were] so bruised that the blood and marrow spouted forth in great abundance'. And yet: 'Despite these torments the doctor never shrunk any whit, neither would he then confess it the sooner, for all the tortures inflicted upon him.'

One would have thought this continued protestation of his innocence would be enough to convince Dr Fian's accusers, but it was not to be. His reward for his courage was to be burned at the stake in 1591.

In complete contrast is the case of Major Weir. Thomas Weir had been an officer in the Parliamentarian army and, in the same year that Charles I was executed in London, he was made Commander of the City Guard of Edinburgh. He shared a mansion in West Bow, Edinburgh, with his unmarried sister Jean. Weir was considered a thoroughly upright and respectable member of the city's establishment and the Presbyterian Church. In the year 1669, however, Major Weir, astonished and horrified his peers by calmly announcing that he was a practising witch and had been so all his life. At the time he was aged 69 or 70. As well as admitting to devil worship, Weir catalogued a list of crimes he had committed, many of them of a sexual nature, including incest and bestiality – 'many things which Christian ears ought not to be defiled with', as one commentator put it.

So shocking and so hard to believe was this testimony that at first it was assumed Major Weir had lost his senses. Several doctors examined him and were pained to admit that he seemed to be entirely rational. To make matters worse, Jean Weir confirmed that she and her brother were in an incestuous relationship and she too was a witch. The magistrates had no choice but to arrest the pair of them. Throughout his trial Major Weir was the personification of arrogance. While incarcerated, he was invited to pray by the chaplain but retorted: 'Torment me not before my time!' Jean Weir babbled out increasingly bizarre statements about their devilish ways. She claimed her brother's walking stick was a sorcerer's wand and that they would both by driven back and forth to Black Masses in a fiery coach.

The Weirs were sentenced to be burned to death in the Grassmarket, close to their home. Given the opportunity to repent before the sentence was carried out, Major Weir refused, saying: 'I lived as a beast and I must die as a beast.' Jean Weir jeered at the crowd, tearing her clothes to show off her breasts, and screamed obscenities as the pyre was lit.

Not surprisingly, these extraordinary events captured the imagination and soon passed into local legend. Both Thomas and Jean Weir were believed to haunt their former home and their place of execution. People spoke of seeing Major Weir's ghost riding through the Grassmarket on a headless horse wreathed in flames. Jean's ghost was said to appear in a particularly ghastly form, her flesh blackened and charred from the flames that took her life.

For years their former home in West Bow stood empty and was avoided by the locals. There was talk of mysterious lights shining from its empty rooms, and some claimed to have seen the phantoms of the Weirs emerging out of the empty mansion and then being driven away in the fiery coach mentioned in Jean's testimony. When one couple did attempt to live in the house, they were frightened away on their first night by the manifestation of a devilish-looking beast in their bedroom. Eventually the house was torn down.

The mansion in West Bow, now demolished, which was home to the self-confessed witches Thomas and Jean Weir.

In the Middle Ages anyone with a bit of learning might be perceived as uncanny. This was certainly true of Michael Scot (sometimes spelled 'Scott'), who was born in Fife in the 12th century and who made a name for himself all over Europe. Scot was a Christian and at one time was offered an archbishopric by Pope Honorius III. But he was also a mathematician, alchemist and astrologer and the author of several books on occult matters, including divination. Science and the occult were greatly intertwined in those days. Scot was as infamous as he was famous, so much so that Dante mentions him by name in his *Divine Comedy* as one of the sorcerers trapped in the Eighth Circle of Hell. He is also namechecked as a magician by Boccaccio.

Scot's legend as an enchanter lingered long in Scottish folklore, where he is often referred to as 'Auld Michael'. Tradition had it he had a host of spirits at his beck and call. Whenever he had guests staying in his castle, these invisible servants would bring delicacies to his table from France and Spain. He fought and vanquished a mighty demon which, to prove its power, split the single peak of Eildon Hill into three. Another story has Scot journeying south of the border to tackle a gang of witches in Cumbria. He caught them on a hillside at their sabbat, dancing in a ring. With his magical powers, he turned them to stone and they are now known as Long Meg and her Daughters (actually a prehistoric stone circle).

Scot died in 1292 and was buried at the Abbey Church of St Mary the Virgin at Melrose. His spirit is said to haunt the abbey ruins in the form of a slithering serpent.

THE HELL CLUB

In addition to Sir Walter Scott's contribution to the propagation of Scottish folklore, there is another author who deserves a mention: Catherine Crowe. Mrs Crowe was a popular novelist of the early and mid-Victorian age who also compiled a fascinating collection of allegedly true experiences with the supernatural, to which she gave the evocative title of *The Night Side of Nature*.

Many of the accounts collected in *The Night Side of Nature* were told to Mrs Crowe personally by the witnesses themselves. They include ghost sightings, spiritualism, prophetic dreams and episodes of second sight. Because Mrs Crowe was living in Edinburgh while writing the work, many of the stories are of Scottish origin. The story of the Glasgow 'Hell Club' is probably apocryphal but is so dramatic that I feel it deserves a place in this volume, and am pleased to present it as originally written, in Mrs Crowe's splendidly Gothic prose:

'Some ninety years ago [i.e. in the 1750s], there flourished in Glasgow a club of young men, which, from the extreme profligacy of its members and the licentiousness of their orgies, was called the "Hell Club". Besides these nightly or weekly meetings, they held one grand annual saturnalia, in which each tried to excel the other in drunkenness and blasphemy; and on these occasions there was no star amongst them whose lurid light was more conspicuous than that of young Mr Archibald B., who, endowed with brilliant talents and a handsome person, had held out great promise in his boyhood, and raised hopes, which had been completely frustrated by his subsequent reckless dissipations.

'One morning, after returning from this annual festival, Mr Archibald B., having retired to bed, dreamt the following dream:

'He fancied that he himself was mounted on a favourite black horse that he always rode, and that he was proceeding towards his own house, then a country seat embowered by trees, and situated on a hill, now entirely built over and forming part of the city, when a stranger, whom the darkness of night prevented his distinctly discerning, suddenly seized his horse's reins, saying, "You must go with me!"

"And who are you?" exclaimed the young man, with a volley of oaths, while he struggled to free himself.

"That you will see by and by," returned the other, in a tone that excited unaccountable terror in the youth, who, plunging his spurs into his horse, attempted to fly. But in vain: however fast the animal flew, the stranger was still beside him, till at length, in his desperate efforts to escape, the rider was thrown, but instead of being dashed to the earth, as he expected, he found himself falling – falling – falling still, as if sinking into the bowels of the earth.

'At length, a period being put to this mysterious descent, he found breath to inquire of his companion, who was still beside him, whither they were going: "Where am I? Where are you taking me?" he exclaimed. "To hell!" replied the stranger, and immediately interminable echoes repeated the fearful sound, "To hell! to hell! to hell!"

'At length a light appeared, which soon increased to a blaze; but instead of the cries, and groans, and lamentings the terrified traveller expected, nothing met his ear but sounds of music, mirth and jollity; and he found himself at the entrance of a superb building, far exceeding any he had seen constructed by human hands. Within, too, what a scene! No amusement, employment, or pursuit of man on earth, but was here being carried on with a vehemence that excited his unutterable amazement.

'There the young and lovely still swam through the mazes of the giddy dance! There the panting steed still bore his brutal rider through the excitement of the goaded race! There, over the midnight bowl, the intemperate still drawled out the wanton song or maudlin blasphemy! The gambler plied for ever his endless game, and the slaves of Mammon toiled through eternity their bitter task; whilst all the magnificence of earth paled before that which now met his view!

'He soon perceived that he was amongst old acquaintances whom he knew to be dead, and each, he observed, was pursuing the object, whatever it was, that had formerly engrossed him; when, finding himself relieved of the presence of his unwelcome conductor, he ventured to address his former friend, Mrs D., whom he saw sitting as had been her wont on earth, absorbed at loo, requesting her to rest from the game, and introduce him to the pleasures of the place, which appeared to him to be very unlike what he had expected and, indeed, an extremely agreeable one.

'But with a cry of agony, she answered, that there was no rest in hell; that they must ever toil on at those very pleasures; and innumerable voices echoed through the interminable vaults, "There is no rest in hell!" Whilst, throwing open their vest, each disclosed in his bosom an ever burning flame! These, they said, were the pleasures of hell; and their choice on earth was now their inevitable doom! In the midst of the horror this scene inspired, his conductor returned, and, at his earnest entreaty, restored him again to earth; but as he quitted him, he said, "Remember; in a year and a day we meet again!"

'At this crisis of his dream the sleeper awoke feverish and ill; and whether from the effects of the dream, or of his preceding orgies, he was so unwell as to be obliged to keep his bed for several days, during which period he had time for many serious reflections, which terminated in a resolution to abandon the club and his licentious companions altogether. He was no sooner well, however, than they flocked around him, bent on recovering so valuable a member of their society; and having wrung from him a confession of the cause of his defection, which, as may be supposed, appeared to them eminently ridiculous, they soon contrived to make him ashamed of his good resolutions.

IStock Photo

The Glasgow Necropolis has become an unexpected tourist attraction. How many members of the so-called 'Hell Club' might be buried here?

'He joined them again, resumed his former course of life, and when the annual saturnalia came round, he found himself with his glass in his hand, at the table, when the president, rising to make the accustomed speech, began by saying, "Gentlemen: this being a leap-year it is a year and a day since our last anniversary," etc. etc. The words struck upon the young man's ear like a knell; but ashamed to expose his weakness to the jeers of his companions, he sat out the feast, plying himself with wine even more liberally than usually, in order to drown his intrusive thoughts; till, in the gloom of a winter's morning he mounted his horse to ride home.

'Some hours afterwards, the horse was found with his saddle and bridle on, quietly gazing by the road-side, about half-way between the city and Mr B's house; whilst a few yards off lay the corpse of his master.'

THE SCENTS OF CULLODEN

Culloden Moor is the site of the last major battle to be fought on British soil (on 16 April 1746) and is certainly one of the most haunted. Phantom soldiers have been seen on the anniversary of the battle, in which the Jacobite forces of Bonnie Prince Charlie were defeated by an army under the command of the Duke of Cumberland.

Strange lights and the sounds of battle have also been reported and one man claimed to have seen a vision of the opposing armies in the sky above the field as he looked out of the window of a passing train. There is also said to be the ghost of a Highlander who mutters the word 'Defeated' before vanishing before the eyes of startled witnesses. St Mary's Well on the battlefield is also said to be haunted by the ghosts of Jacobites.

One visitor to the battlefield related how she had noticed that a square of Stuart tartan cloth had been blown down from a memorial stone and onto a grave. She picked it up, intending to replace it, only to see lying beneath it the prone body of a handsome young Highlander. Realising she was witnessing something uncanny, she fled the field. The ghost of Bonnie Prince Charlie himself, dressed in green tartan, is said to haunt nearby Culloden House.

Arguably the strangest phenomenon connected to Culloden is the 'Scents', as highlighted in a booklet published by the Edinburgh Psychic College in the 1940s. A member of the college reproduced

a letter she had received about mysterious aromas detected on the moor. The anonymity of the witness was retained. She wrote:
'Ten years ago [around 1937], my sister and I were staying in Inverness, and went to Culloden Moor. Our mother was a Calder, and her family were out in the risings of '15 and '45. Culloden Moor is the saddest place I have ever seen. I could almost hear the weeping and wailing that must have taken place there, and going to every cairn said a De Profundis at each one. Presently, I caught the scent of roses or sweet peas or other flowers, but there was nothing to account for the scent, no flowers anywhere. Next I could smell incense, and last of all a smell of burning wood.

'In spite of looking everywhere, and in every direction, there was no sign of anything whatsoever to account for the scents. I was puzzled. Next day, I crossed to Skye, and not long afterwards I picked up a very old magazine, left lying about by another guest. In turning the leaves I was petrified with amazement to read an article entitled "The Scents of Culloden Moor". The writer mentions the scent of flowers, of burning pastilles (incense).

'I have one thing to add to this. I went to the memorial service on April 16 this year and had I experienced any sensation of scents that day, I should not have been at all surprised, as I was very worked up. It is a most moving ceremony. But I felt nothing. Sometime in May, I rode out taking ten small children, all on bikes, to visit the battlefield. After I'd shoo'ed them off, I stopped behind to look round to see they'd left no mess, and no one had lingered, heaved a sigh of relief at having done this when I was bathed in a wave of most glorious scent – the hot sweet scent of a garden in full bloom. For a moment, I didn't think, but I looked around in surprise to see from whence it came, as it was early in the season.

'Suddenly I realised I was in the middle of the moor and no garden near, and I also realised that utterly unexpectedly I had experienced the "Scents". I had, unfortunately, no time to linger and see if they were followed up by any of the other scents. And though I have been back once or twice, that is the only time in which I experienced it. I have ancestors buried there. I belong to the Church of Scotland. But I am of Highland descent, and I'm considered very psychic, as I have dreams of dreams and seen visions.'

One of the memorials on the Battlefield of Culloden. Many people have had spooky experiences on Culloden Moor.

IStock Photo

SCOTTISH GHOST-LORE

Scotland has a spectacularly rich heritage of ghost stories. I have already presented many of these in the companion volume to this work, *Scottish Ghost Stories* (Bradwell 2013), and only have room to mention a few here.

Alasdair Alpin MacGregor, an author already mentioned in relation to the Iona 'time slip' (see the 'Holy Lore' chapter), devotes a whole chapter of his *Ghost Book* to 'Phantom Lights' seen in Scotland. These are Scottish versions of phenomena which appear in folklore throughout the British Isles. In England they are given names such as 'spook lights', 'punkie lights', 'Lantern Men' and 'Jack o' Lantern.' In Wales they were known as *canwyllau cyrff*, which means 'corpse candles'. In Gaelic such a light is called a *gealbhan* or 'ball of fire'.

Often the mysterious little lights would appear outside the rooms or houses of people who were about to die. Alternatively, they might be seen floating down the lanes towards the local burial ground, taking the route soon to be followed by a funeral procession of someone in the community.

MacGregor was told an interesting example of this phenomenon by a man named Morrison, a native of the Isle of Lewis in the Outer Hebrides. One night Morrison was returning from Stornoway in a pony and trap driven by the son of the farmer at Stoneyfield. When they reached a crossroads not far from Stoneyfield Farm,

Morrison jumped down, because his home was along one of the lanes, and the farmer's son continued on his way. Tramping down the lane, Morrison happened to glance over his shoulder, and was surprised to see a strange light travelling in front of the trap. It remained hovering in front of the horses until the trap disappeared from his view.

The next morning Morrison asked the farmer's son whether he had seen the light. He had — and had followed it for some distance, past his destination, only to lose sight of it when it appeared to turn in at a neighbouring farm. The farmer's boy was so mystified that he had knocked up the household at the farm to ask them whether they knew of anyone who might have arrived there, possibly on horseback and carrying a bright lantern. He was told — rather crossly, I suspect — that anyone belonging to the farm was in bed. A day or two later it became clear that the light the two young men had seen was of supernatural origin. Tragedy visited the farm where the *gealbhan* disappeared. The old farmer was drowned in Stornoway harbour. His body was carried home to the farm in the Stoneyfield farmer's trap.

In Scotland the ghostly lights also haunted the sites of past tragedies. When MacGregor was staying in Skye, researching a book on that fascinating isle, he spoke to another visitor, an Edinburgh doctor, who had seen a *gealbhan* only a few evenings before. He had gone out for an evening stroll from the inn where he was staying at Broadford, and had noticed it shining far out in the bay. At first, he told MacGregor, he assumed it was a light on a fishing boat, but soon realised that couldn't be the case because it was approaching him across the water far too swiftly and smoothly. He described it as a 'globe of light — a light such as one might see hanging from a lamp-standard in a modern city'.

When the light reached the water's edge, something even weirder occurred. The light went out and in its place the doctor glimpsed the apparition of a woman carrying a baby in her arms. The figure hurried across the sands, then it too vanished. The doctor later learned a story to account for his experience. The landlord at the inn told him that, several years before, the bodies of a dead woman and a dead child were found washed up from a shipwreck at the very spot on the shore where he had seen the apparition.

The strangest example of this phenomenon is arguably the one described in *The Ghosts, Spirits and Spectres of Scotland* by Francis Thompson. This was a shaft of golden light which haunted a house in Ayr. It emitted the smell of heliotropes. The light commemorated the murder of a young woman by burglars. The room where she was killed was taken down and a garden was planted in its place. This was planted with her favourite flowers: the heliotrope.

Related to these ghostly lights are phantom funerals, another apparition common in folklore across the UK. These would take the exact likeness of a real funeral that was shortly to take place, but would usually appear at night. It was best to keep to the verges when using country lanes after dark, especially those which led to graveyards, in case a phantom funeral should suddenly manifest. It was possible to get caught up in the apparition and be dragged along with it. Here is Francis Thompson's account of one such incident:

'A man in Sutherland was walking home one night when, as he neared his house, he began to wonder why the house was just as far away with every step he took. To his surprise and dismay he found himself in a churchyard quite some distance from his home. He could hear distinctly the noise of a spade working among earth, stones and gravel. He knew then that he must have been caught up

A mystified traveller follows a gealbhan, or phantom ball of light.

by a phantom funeral and carried to the churchyard. Later, when he got home, he heard that a neighbour woman had seen a ghostly funeral on the same road which the man had taken to walk home, thus obtaining a first-hand confirmation of his own experience.'

There are many famous haunted locations throughout Scotland. They include Glamis Castle, Tayside, said to be haunted by the fearsome, hirsute form of Earl Beardie; the surprisingly gentle presence of a woman burned as a witch; and a number of other apparitions, including those of a little black boy and a figure who hurries through the gardens and is known as 'Jack the Runner'. Glamis also has the abiding legend of a locked room in which resides a mysterious, immortal monster.

Other famously 'ghosted' castles include Traquair, in the Borders, haunted by Bonnie Prince Charlie; Cortachy, in Angus, haunted by a cruelly treated drummer boy; Spedlins Tower, in Dumfries and Galloway, where the eerie groans of a starving prisoner may still be heard; and Hermitage Castle, in the Borders, which is haunted by 'Bad Lord Soulis', whose tyranny eventually led to him being dropped into a cauldron of boiling water by his subjects.

Edinburgh Castle has numerous ghosts. These include another drummer boy, a prisoner who died in an escape attempt, a Lady of Glamis, and spectral cats and dogs, to say nothing of the dismal moans heard in the castle vaults. Edinburgh is certainly one of the most haunted cities in Britain. A stroll down the Royal Mile will take you past numerous haunted houses and pubs, and on the streets themselves you might encounter a phantom coach or the apparition of a Civil War general on a galloping horse. Towards the end is a government building called Queensberry House. This is possessed of the frail ghost of a servant boy, who was cooked and eaten by a crazed cannibal. Holyrood Palace, at the very end of the Royal Mile, is haunted by a Grey Lady and a man dressed in the fashions of the 16th century.

Elsewhere in Edinburgh, allegedly haunted locations can be met with at almost every turn. One of the best known is Greyfriars Kirkyard, where scores of 'Covenanters', people seeking religious independence in the 17th century, were locked up on suspicion of treason. They were treated so barbarically that many of these men, women and children died. Today the graveyard has a decidedly eerie reputation, with many visitors claiming to feel an overwhelming sense of dread in the area where the Covenanters were imprisoned. A weird glowing figure has also purportedly been seen here. The cemetery is also famous for 'Greyfriars Bobby', the

IStock Photo

Historic Glamis Castle is one of the most famously haunted places in Scotland.

little terrier who refused to quit his master's grave: a neat bronze statue commemorates him.

Glasgow also has its ghosts and its magnificently creepy Victorian graveyard, the Southern Necropolis in the Gorbals, has a particularly spooky reputation. Here it is said a statue on one of the memorials has a habit of turning its head and watching people as they pass by!

All these places, and many more, are described in more detail in my *Scottish Ghost Stories*. I shall therefore end on an unusual little ghost story which does not appear in that book. A young man who worked at a shooting lodge in the North West Highlands was having his hair cut by a coachman, when the latter noticed

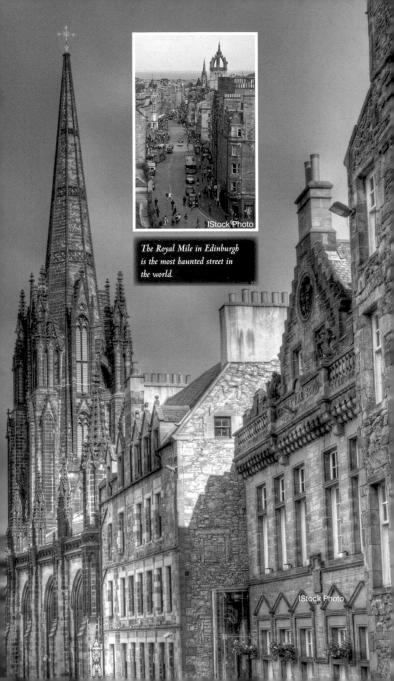

The Royal Mile in Edinburgh is the most haunted street in the world.

something worrying: a lump was growing out of the side of the youth's head. He mentioned it and the young man grew pale. He said that the discovery proved that his life was in danger, for the lump was evidence of a curse placed upon him by a ghost!

He explained to the startled company that a few evenings previously he had been crossing over the hill called Cnoc-na-Moine when, in a hollow near the top, his way was barred by a grim-visaged Highlander. The man glared at the storyteller, who, knowing that this particular hollow had an eerie reputation, realised he was face to face with a spirit. It is a common theme in ghost-lore that earth-bound spirits cannot speak until spoken to, and even then only if charged to do so in religious terms. In Gaelic, the brave youngster piped up: 'In the name of the Trinity, if you come from heaven or hell, and have anything to say, I shall listen.'

The phantom replied: 'I was murdered on this very spot 124 years ago, and I am allowed to visit once a year ever since on the anniversary of the murder to tell it to someone ere I can be allowed to rest in the place I have been sent to. I could never meet anyone before who spoke to me, and I want to tell you that I was coming home from the south with some money, when two brothers of the name of A., who lived at B., set on me, killed me, took my money and then buried my body.

'As my people did not know that I was coming the murderers were never found out, and were never suspected to be what they were. They built a good house with the money, and their descendants occupy it to this day, and now I want you to tell the people of the place who murdered me.'

The terrified youth was loath to spread this story, for Mr A. would not like to hear such a tale of his ancestor and would

certainly not believe it. It would undoubtedly cause trouble in the neighbourhood, and for the storyteller in particular. But the ghost would brook no refusal. It continued: 'If you don't tell, you will find that I can do you harm. You will find that if you keep my secret, soon a lump will begin to grow on your head and will press on your brain so that you will become mad, and in your madness you will tell the secret. It is better for you to tell it before that happens.'

With that bleak warning, the phantom Highlander sank back into the earth and the troubled boy continued on his way. Now that the deadly lump had manifested on his head, he realised he had no choice but to repeat the ghost's story. The young man did not go mad and the lump on his head subsided now that he had discharged his duty. Although the tale spread through the neighbourhood, the families of the deceased Highlander and his alleged murderers did not come to blows, as might have been expected. Everyone shrugged it off and got on with their lives. Any revenge looked for by the murdered Highlander therefore did not come to pass, but he was never more seen in the spooky hollow on Cnoc-na-Moine.

ALSO FROM RICHARD HOLLAND FOR BRADWELL BOOKS

LEGENDS & FOLKLORE
Nottinghamshire
Wales
Wiltshire

GHOST STORIES
Cambridgeshire
Cheshire
Cotswolds
Cumbrian
Dorset
Essex
Hampshire & the Isle of Wight
Kent
Lancashire
London
Norfolk
North Wales
Oxfordshire
Scottish
Somerset
South Wales
Surrey
Sussex
Yorkshire

BY OTHER AUTHORS
Black Country & Birmingham
(Brendan Hawthorne)
Cornish (A Corn)
Derbyshire (Jill Armitage)
Leicestershire (David Bell)

London Underground (Jill Armitage)
Staffordshire (David Bell)
Welsh Celebrity Ghost Stories (South Wales Paranormal Research)

FROM RICHARD HOLLAND IN 2015/16

LEGENDS & FOLKLORE
Cambridgeshire
Hampshire
Dorset
Somerset

GHOST STORIES
Dorset
Herefordshire
Norfolk
Shropshire
Somerset
Warwickshire
Northumberland
Nottinghamshire
Devon
Lincolnshire

For more information visit
www.bradwellbooks.com